THE OLYMPICS

ANCIENT OLYMPIC GAMES

REVISED AND UPDATED

Haydn Middleton

Heinemann LIBRARY

H **www.heinemann.co.uk/library**
Visit our website to find out more information about Heinemann Library books.

To order:
☎ Phone 44 (0) 1865 888066
▤ Send a fax to 44 (0)1865 314091
▣ Visit the Heinemann Library Bookshop at www.heinemann.co.uk/library to browse our catalogue and order online.

First published in Great Britain by Heinemann Library, Halley Court, Jordan Hill, Oxford OX2 8EJ, part of Harcourt Education.
Heinemann Library is a registered trademark of Harcourt Education Ltd.

Editorial: Joanna Talbot
Design: Philippa Jenkins
Picture Research: Tracy Cummins
Production: Alison Parsons

Originated by Modern Age
Printed and bound in China by Leo Paper Group

ISBN 978 0 431 19158 4
12 11 10 09 08
10 9 8 7 6 5 4 3 2 1

British Library Cataloguing in Publication Data
Middleton, Haydn
    Ancient Olympic Games. – (The Olympics)
    1. Olympic games (Ancient) – Juvenile literature
    2. Greece civilization – Juvenile literature
    I. Title.
    796.4·8·0938

A full catalogue record for this book is available from the British Library.

Acknowledgements
The Publishers would like to thank the following for permission to reproduce photographs:
AKG London: E Lessing p. 13; Allsport: p. 8; Ancient Art and Architecture Collection Ltd: pp. 6, 7, 10, 11, 12, 19, 23, 25; AP Photo/Marco Trovati p. 29; Ashmolean Museum, Oxford: p. 20; British Museum: p. 17; C M Dixon: pp. 14, 18, 24; Corbis: pp. 4 (Tim de Waele), 28 (Stapleton Collection); Hirmer Fotoarchiv: p. 22; Michael Holford: pp. 15, 17, 21; Kobal Collection: p. 26; Scala: Galleria Borghese p. 27.

Cover photograph reproduced with permission of Evelyn De Morgan/Getty Images.

The publishers would like to thank John Townsend for his assistance with the preparation of this book.

Every effort has been made to contact copyright holders of any material reproduced in this book. Any omissions will be rectified in subsequent printings if notice is given to the publishers.

CONTENTS

Any words appearing in the text in bold, **like this**, are explained in the Glossary.

INTRODUCTION

What do you think about when you hear the words 'Olympic Games'? Spectacular festivals of sport? Huge crowds of spectators? Grand ceremonies and processions? For many people, these scenes come to mind whenever the Olympic Games are mentioned. But what else do we know?

Well, only men are allowed to take part in any of the events, and they must be naked. Almost any woman found in the stadium, even just to watch, can be executed. On the second day, there are chariot races. On the third, 100 oxen are slaughtered. On the fourth, athletes take part in a combat sport where they are expected to break each other's fingers…

Does any of this seem strange? It should do! That second paragraph describes the original Olympic Games – first held in Greece more than 2,500 years ago. But the scenes in the first paragraph also describe those very first Olympics. Just like our modern Olympic Games, the ancient Olympics were great, popular sporting events. Even so, there are many differences between the Olympics of ancient Greece and those of the 21st century.

KEEPING FIT

The Greeks had practical reasons for keeping fit and playing sport. According to the Greek writer Xenophon:

"A good citizen must keep himself in good condition, ready to serve his state at a moment's notice. The instinct of self-preservation demands it likewise: for how helpless is the state of the ill-trained youth in war or in danger! Finally, what a disgrace it is for a man to grow old without ever seeing the beauty and the strength of which his body is capable!"

▶ In 2004, the Olympic Games returned to Greece. The opening ceremony in Athens was a far cry from the first Olympic Games.

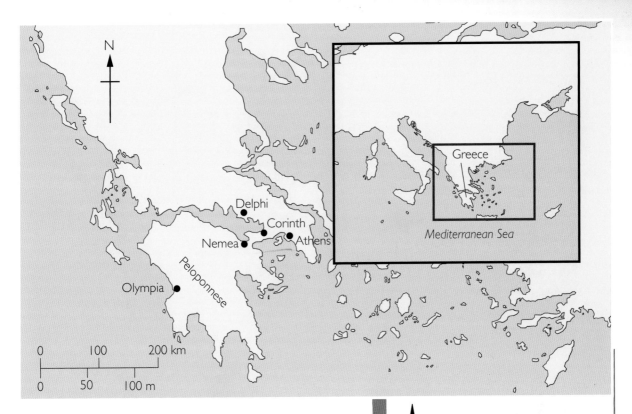

HEROIC BEGINNINGS

The ancient Games were held every four years at a place called Olympia – to honour the great Greek god Zeus. According to tradition, the first Olympic champion was Coroebus of Elis, a local cook. He won the sprint race in 776BC. By that time, the Games were probably about 500 years old already. (That, at least, is the belief of **archaeologists** who have **excavated** at Olympia; there are no reliable written records.) The ancient Greeks, who loved their **myths** and **legends**, claimed that the hero Hercules was the Games' **founder**.

▲ Olympia was not exactly a *town* in ancient Greece – more like a great sports centre combined with an important place of worship. It lay within the **city state** of Elis, on an area of land known as the Peloponnese. In ancient times Greece was not a single country but a collection of city states which were often fierce rivals.

We do know that, after 776BC, the Games continued for more than 1,000 years. On the following pages, you can read about some of the things that happened at Olympia in this very long period of time. As you will see, much of our information comes from books written while the Games were still going on. Other evidence has been dug up by archaeologists. Many of the pictures in this book show statues and vase paintings that were made in ancient times and which give us important evidence about the sports and sportsmen of the ancient Olympic Games.

FAR MORE THAN A GAME

Many people nowadays take sport very seriously. To them it is almost like a religion. Well, in ancient Greece sport *was* a religion! Athletic festivals, or games, were held as a way of worshipping Zeus and the other gods. The biggest of these festivals was the Olympic Games.

A SPORTING CALENDAR

In ancient Greece athletic games could be held at funerals, in memory of the dead. They were also arranged as celebrations for heroes. But, above all, they were staged in honour of the gods and goddesses who, the ancient Greeks believed, held people's lives in the palms of their hands.

Greek athletic festivals ranged in size from small contests for local people up to great, regular, national meetings which drew competitors and spectators from far and wide in the ancient world. These national meetings played such an important part in Greek life that people made the period of years from one Games until the next into a unit of time. The four-year period between each Olympic Games was known as an 'Olympiad'.

Remains from ancient Greek art show that many battles were fought. Even so, wars were put 'on hold' for three months to let the Olympic Games go ahead. City states which were at war with one another could send their athletes to take part in safety. No such truce exists for the modern Olympics. In 1916, and again in 1940 and 1944, the Games were not held while World Wars One and Two were raging.

Only a rich area could afford its own stadium and all the facilities needed to stage important Games. The four top-ranking games took place in four major centres:

Olympia   (Olympic Games)

Delphi   (Pythian Games)

Corinth   (Isthmian Games)

Nemea   (Nemean Games)

EYES ON THE PRIZES

The Pythian Games, like the Olympics, were held every four years; the others took place every two years. These 'period Games' were sometimes known as 'Sacred Crown Games'. This was because the winners received only wreaths, or crowns, to mark their victories. The wreaths at Olympia were made of olive leaves, at Delphi they were made of laurel with a handful of apples, at Corinth they were made of pine or sometimes **celeriac**, and at Nemea they were also made of celeriac.

But the athletes at these Games were not pure **amateurs**. When the victors returned to their own **city states**, they were given more practical rewards – like sums of money, which could be very large. Wealthy citizens were often glad to feed and entertain famous victors (winners), and threw big parties for them. An athlete who won at all four major festivals was also given the special Greek title of *periodonikes*, which meant that he was a multiple champion.

Athena, daughter of Zeus, was the guardian goddess of Athens. Its people held games called the *Panathenaia* in her honour. Winners and runners-up there were rewarded with very precious prizes of olive oil. The oil was taken from a tree that Athena herself was supposed to have planted.

THE GHOST STADIUM OF OLYMPIA

The Olympia Stadium was not built in a city but beside a holy **sanctuary** dedicated to the Greek god Zeus. It was here that many of the ancient Games were staged, with crowds coming from all over Greece and beyond.

THE RUIN

After the Romans took control of Greece, the ancient Games began to change, before being stopped (see pages 26-27). The whole site at Olympia fell into disuse and the walls crumbled. For almost 1,500 years the area, between two rivers, became overgrown and was covered by a swamp. It was not until 1829 that French **archaeologists** began digging for the remains of the stadium. Instead, they uncovered the Temple of Zeus. It took a much longer **excavation** from 1875 to 1881 by a German team to uncover the whole site. They found the stadium, which was later restored – so that visitors today can really imagine how the ancient Games looked. If they listen hard, visitors might even hear the ghostly echoes of cheers from more than 1,500 years ago!

◀ This is how the gateway to the stadium at Olympia looks today. Once it was teeming with people.

STADIUM STATISTICS

Archaeologists have shown that the stadium at Olympia was built about 2,500 years ago. They also found some other interesting facts:

- The stadium held up to 45,000 spectators who sat on steep banks of earth on three sides of the track. There were no stone seats, just a box where the chief judges sat.

- Opposite the judges' box there was an altar to the goddess Demeter Chamyne. The unmarried priestess of this goddess and maidens (unmarried women) were the only women allowed to watch the Games.

- During the Games, the spectators slept out in the open at night.

TRACK FACTS

The running track was 193 metres (630 feet) long and 32 metres (105 feet) wide. Twenty runners could use the track at the same time. A low wall separated the spectators from the track. Stone starting lines that were one *stade* (192.28 metres/627.5 feet) apart marked the course at each end.

The site of Olympia looked like this from above. At the centre is the sacred **precinct**, known as the *Altis*, or Grove of Zeus. Measuring more than 180 m along each side, it contained the temples of Zeus and Hera (his wife) and other official buildings.

Outside were the stadium itself, the **hippodrome** where horse-races were held (no trace of this has been found, but a writer called Pausanias described it in detail) and the *palaestra* where combat sports were practised.

Until 472BC all the contests took place on one day. Later, they were spread over four days with a fifth devoted to the closing ceremony, presentation of prizes and a banquet for the champions.

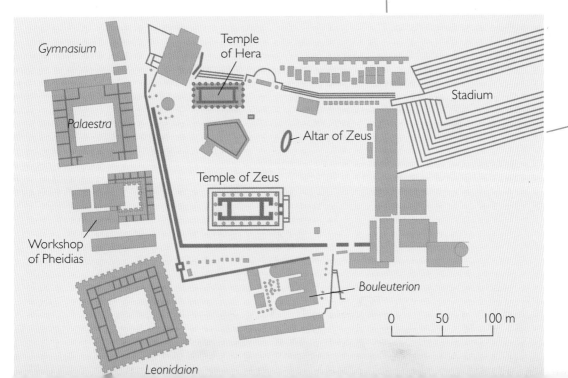

Gymnasium

Temple of Hera

Palaestra

Altar of Zeus

Temple of Zeus

Stadium

Workshop of Pheidias

Bouleuterion

Leonidaion

0   50   100 m

MORE THAN RACES

For many years the ancient Olympic Games had only one event: sprinting. These races ran for just one length of the track (a *stade*). In time, longer races were added, including the *diaulos* (two lengths) and the long-distance *dolichos* race of about 5 kilometres (3.1 miles).

One of the races had to be run in full battle armour. None of the other runners had to worry about getting so hot, as they wore no clothes at all. As the Games became more popular, more events were added. Even so, there was nothing like the number of sports included in the modern Olympics. Over the last 100 years, more and more sports have been added, so that in the 2008 Olympics in Beijing, the number of different heats and matches are expected to reach a record number, with over 300 final competitions.

WINNER TAKES ALL?

These days all Olympic runners' performances are timed with great accuracy – although beating their fellow athletes to the gold medal is still the most important thing. At the ancient Games athletes raced only against one another, not against a clock.

Running in armour was more like a novelty race than a serious contest. But it reminded spectators of the original reason for the Games – to train the competitors for war.

To them, all that mattered was the honour and glory of victory – whatever the winning margin. Since 1908, the modern Games' unofficial motto has been this: 'The most important thing in the Olympic Games is not to win but to take part, just as the most important thing in life is not the triumph but the struggle.' Athletes at ancient Olympia would have been baffled by that idea. It also seems to be **alien** to many people involved in sport today. ('It's not the winning' – as an advertisement for one sporting goods manufacturer recently proclaimed – 'it's the taking apart!')

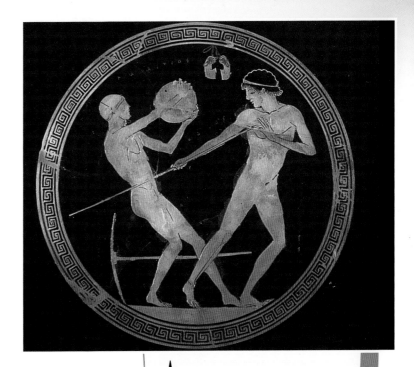

This picture from the 4th century BC shows athletes throwing the discus and javelin.

Winning any contest was important, but not winning at all costs. Competitors and officials alike had to take an oath to stick closely to the rules and neither to offer nor take bribes. Cheating of any kind was severely punished – sometimes by special whipping-men who were kept on stand-by. Fines for wrongdoing paid for *zanes* (bronze statues of Zeus) to be built. The row of these on display at the entrance to Olympia reminded new arrivals that they were always under the great god's eye. Even that was not enough to stop some cheats from bending the rules, but it seems that foul play and bribery were not common.

FIELD OF HONOUR

As well as track events, the stadium spectators could enjoy 'field' sports like jumping – long, but not high – and throwing the discus or the javelin. There was also a five-event contest known as the **pentathlon**. The olive-wreath winner of that sport had to run, jump, throw both discus and javelin, *and* wrestle.

WRESTLING WONDERS

Wrestling was extremely popular in ancient Greece. The right way to wrestle was taught at many special schools – and ordinary people as well as **professionals** loved to take part in this very old sport. The best wrestlers of all competed at the Olympic and other Sacred Crown Games. Some of them were so mighty – and so popular with the crowds and with writers – that we still know their feats and names today.

MILO OF CROTON

An early Olympic superstar was a wrestler called Milo the Giant, from the Greek **colony** of Croton in southern Italy. He won at Olympia as a boy, probably in 540BC, and then another five times as an adult. He also won 25 crowns at the other three Sacred Games, over a period of at least 24 years.

Modern wrestlers and boxers must compete in 'classes' depending on their weight. In ancient times there were age divisions but no weight classes. This led to some great feats of eating because the bigger and stronger you were, the better.

According to reports, Milo of Croton ate 9 kg (20 lbs) of meat and 9 kg (20 lbs) of bread each day, and washed it down with 9 litres (19 pints) of wine. Once he carried a four-year-old bull around the stadium at Olympia before eating it all in the course of a single day! ▼

Milo could stand on an oiled discus and stay on it, however hard anyone tried to push him off. He was also said to tie a string around his temples, then make the veins there swell up so much that they broke it. And the writer Diodorus Siculus described how he once led his countrymen to victory against a far larger army from Sybaris. Apparently, he came to the battle wearing his Olympic crowns.

As with more modern popular heroes, some of the stories told about Milo seem a little far-fetched. This was how he was supposed to have met his death: while out walking in the countryside, he found a partly split tree, with wedges still stuck into the springy wood. He tried to pull the tree completely apart, but when the wedges fell out, the tree snapped tightly shut on his hands. He could not free himself and, in the end, wolves came and finished him off.

FOOD FOR FIGHTING

Astyanax of Miletus, a regular wrestling winner at the Games, was famous for his enormous appetite. Once at a party he was said to have offered to eat everyone's food by himself – then went ahead and did so. His bones were so big that after he died they did not fit into the large jar in which human remains used to be buried. His family had to supply a second jar!

Most wrestling scenes in Greek art show the standing part of the bout, rather than ground-fighting – although both were traditional features of the sport. Ancient wrestling could be skilful and scientific.

A Sicilian Greek, Leontiskos, won at Olympia in the mid 5th century BC even though he could not throw his opponents. So how did he succeed? He broke their fingers! ▼

BRILLIANT BOXERS

Boxing was the other combat sport of ancient Greece. But there were several differences between the sport then and now. There was no ring, for example, nor was there any point scoring – you either won or you lost. Bouts went on until one man accepted defeat by holding up a finger or was simply knocked out cold. Sometimes winning came at a high cost: any boxer killed during a contest was proclaimed the victor, while his killer was turned away from the stadium.

BOXING IN THE BLOOD

Great sporting ability often passes from one generation of a family to the next. This was certainly true of Diagoras of Rhodes (5th century BC), his sons and grandsons. Diagoras' own great-grandfather was a king, but according to the great Greek writer Aristotle, he also had the blood of *gods* in his veins: Hermes, the messenger god, was said to have been his father. A man of enormous size and a supreme boxer, he became a **periodonikes** by winning at each of the Sacred Crown Games, as well as at many other festivals.

His sons Akousilaos, Damagetos, and Dorieus all won Olympic crowns after him. And his daughters Pherenike and Kallipateira each produced sons who went on to win Olympic crowns in their turn. Kallipateira even won fame herself – by becoming one of the few married women who actually saw an Olympics and lived to tell the tale.

This magnificent statue of a boxer was made in the 1st century BC. You can see his hands wrapped in sharp **thongs**, which were the ancient alternative to modern boxing gloves. His face and ear show scars inflicted by someone else with similar wrappings!

Boxers had to play it fair and square. Clinching and gripping an opponent's arm were both forbidden. Officials armed with sticks made sure competitors remembered that! ▶

Six victory statues of Diagoras and his descendants were put on display at Olympia. We know about them because parts of the **inscriptions** on them have survived until today.

BRAIN OVER BRAWN

The Greeks liked to think that boxing was an art. They told a **legend** that, at the first Olympic festival, the unlikely champion Apollo (the god of music and art) defeated Ares (the god of war) at boxing. To them, real champions fought with their brains as much as their fists.

A man called Onomastos, from Smyrna, is believed to have drawn up the rules for boxing, some time before 688BC. Another man from the same part of Greece, the stylish Pythagoras of Samos, showed that brains were as important as brute force – triumphing through skill and intelligence. In 588BC he arrived at the Games and applied to box in the boys' division. Laughed at for being too old, he entered the men's division – and won.

But if Olympic boxing still makes you feel squeamish and you do not share the ancient Greeks' belief that it was a thing of beauty – do not turn over and read about another 'heavy sport'. It is not for those of a nervous disposition!

PETRIFYING PANKRATION

Have you ever heard the expression 'no holds barred'? It means that anything goes – you can use any method you like to achieve your goal. *Pankration* (meaning complete strength or complete victory) was an ancient Olympic combat sport in which almost no holds were barred. Strangleholds, kicking, breaking fingers, dislocating limbs – each of these was used in the attempt to put your opponent down. It was an all-out fight, and the writer Pindar recognised this: 'One must wipe out one's rival by doing everything,' he calmly observed.

Perhaps not surprisingly, *pankration* contests attracted very large crowds of spectators. Champion *pankratiasts* like Theagenes of Thasos won undying fame. Just as nowadays the winner of the 100 metres sprint is called the Fastest Man on Earth, so the winner of the *pankration* crown could have been called the Toughest (or maybe just the Nastiest!).

SUPERSTAR

Theagenes of Thasos was a top celebrity. He was such a successful boxer and *pankratiast* that he was worshipped as a god after his death. He won between 1,200 and 1,400 fights over many years, including three Olympic crowns in 480 and 476 BC. According to one **legend**, a statue of Theagenes was set up but one of his old opponents was so bitter that he tried to deface it. The statue promptly toppled over and crushed him to death!

In Sparta, biting and eye-gouging were allowed, but at national festivals they were forbidden in *pankration*. ▼

This vase painting from about the 5th century BC shows two *pankratiasts* in combat. The trainer is about to strike a man with his stick for committing a foul. ▶

PRIME PANKRATIASTIC QUALITIES

Top *pankratiasts* tended to be big men. It was said that the first victor, Lygdamis of Syracuse, was a giant who stood on feet 45 centimetres (18 inches) long. Such champions had to be determined as well as strong. There was no time limit to the exhausting fights except nightfall, so *kartereia* or endurance was a good quality to have. Sometimes it could even be enough to secure a victory.

Amazingly, though, the Greeks thought boxing was the more dangerous sport. An athlete who wanted to compete in both events at Olympia asked for the *pankration* to be held first, so that he would not come to his second contest too badly wounded. And according to one belief, if you dreamed about *pankration*, that was a bad omen. But if you dreamed about boxing, that was even worse – because it meant you were going to suffer bodily harm!

EYEWITNESS REPORT

'I witnessed once in a *pankration* contest,' wrote Philo of Alexandria, 'a man who hurled blows with hands and feet, all of them well-directed, leaving nothing undone that might bring him victory, but who gave up, worn out, and finally left the stadium uncrowned. The man being battered, on the other hand, was compact with solid flesh, ... like a stone or like iron – he didn't give in to the blows and broke the force of his opponent by the toughness of his endurance until he won the final victory.'

HORSEPLAY

Equestrian or horse-riding events were introduced into the modern Olympic Games at Paris in 1900. In the 21st century, there are various individual and team equestrian events, involving **dressage**, show-jumping, and three-day eventing. Horses also played an important part in the ancient Olympics. However, horse sports were very different then.

This **relief** shows a Roman chariot race.

HIP-HIP-HIPPO!

Way back in time, chariot races were a feature of 'Funeral Games'. These marked the deaths of great Greek men. When festival Games began at Olympia, chariot-racing was also included there. This took place in a different building from the stadium, called the **hippodrome**. (*Hippos* is the Greek word for horse.) If you have ever seen the chariot-race scene in the old film *Ben Hur*, about ancient Rome, you will know how thrilling these races could be. The crowds hit a fever pitch of excitement – not just at the skilful charioteering, but also at the spectacular crashes and pile-ups.

Racing horses were expensive to keep and train – and you needed two or four of them to pull a chariot. Rich horse-owners hired jockeys and charioteers to do the actual racing, which could be extremely dangerous. In the 5th century BC, Damonon of Sparta and his son were successful owners who also occasionally raced themselves. But they were an exception.

HORSES FOR COURSES

Racing chariots were not like the sturdy vehicles used in ancient warfare. They were lightweight carriages with two big wheels. The drivers stood well back, over the axle, and held the reins in their hands. (In Roman races, the reins were tied behind their backs, so they had no way of getting the horse to 'brake'. This meant that the races would be faster but more dangerous.) For a while too, mule-cart racing was popular. Mules are a cross between a horse and a donkey, and were normally used for pulling heavy loads.

The age of the racing animals was important, since there were separate races for full-grown horses and younger 'colts'. Horse judges examined the creatures closely before and after races, and horse-doctors were on call for health problems. And, as in all Olympic sports, there had to be fair play at all times. After a judge called Troilus put in some horses and colts for Olympic competitions, and won in both classes, judges were banned from entering their own animals.

IT'S MY EMPIRE AND I'LL RACE IF I WANT TO

Holders of Olympic crowns were famous far and wide. As ancient Greece fell under the control of Rome, many Romans took a great interest in the Games. The unpredictable Emperor Nero decided to compete himself when he visited Greece in AD67.

First he made the Olympic officials change the date of the whole festival, then he entered a chariot race. He was thrown to the ground and did not complete the course. But the nervous officials gave him the crown anyway – since he surely would have won if he had not fallen.

Thus Nero's dream came true: he had won immortality as an Olympic victor. Or had he? When he was dead, the judges at Olympia thought again. They cancelled the festival of AD67 from the records, thus removing Nero's name from the list of winners.

GETTING IN SHAPE

As you will have gathered by now, sport in ancient Greece was a serious business. Whether you were a runner, combat athlete or charioteer, you could not simply turn up at the Olympic Games and hope for the best. Nor could you easily do another job in between festivals. This was because you had to put in long periods of specialist training, paying particular attention to what you ate and drank. If you then succeeded at the Games, you received the rewards of fortune and fame – ancient Olympic champions were like modern football and movie stars rolled into one.

ANCIENT GREEK SPORTS CENTRES

Combat athletes practised at a *palaestra*. From around the 5th century BC, a bigger sports complex called a *gymnasion* was built in many towns and cities. These places were usually open to the public and included a *palaestra*, a covered running track, playing fields, baths, and an altar for making **sacrifices** to the gods.

This scene from an ancient Greek cup shows what went on in a *palaestra* – a place where combat sports were practised.

The two young men on the left are wrestling, watched by a trainer. He holds a stick, which he would not be afraid to use! On the far right a boxer starts to wrap his hands with **thongs**, while next to him an athlete is using a pickaxe to soften up the ground where he will exercise – there were areas of softened sand and mud for wrestlers to practise on. ▼

Greek athletes took food seriously, as shown on ancient vases and water jars. Most people in ancient Greece ate only barley bread, fruit, cheese, vegetables, and perhaps some fish. Top wrestlers, however, gorged on joints of mutton, lamb, **venison**, and beef to put on extra weight and muscle. Without the gifts showered on them by their fans and admirers, many wrestlers could not have afforded so rich a diet. Their meat diet was supplemented by a strict schedule of rest and exercise.

◀

Fans liked to come and watch their athletic heroes training, and also to get themselves fit. The ancient Greeks were very keen on physical fitness. They saw the human body as a thing of great beauty, and they believed – as we do – that exercise could improve mental health as well. Sports watchers saw a link between the way an athlete looked and the way he competed. Types popularly known as the 'Eagle', for example, were fierce and strong but might give in when the going got tough. The 'Bear' was slow but difficult to budge.

Whether they were Eagles, Bears or even 'Pieces of String' (sinewy and lithe), athletes preparing for the Olympics would spend months in training to reach the qualifying standard. Then they had to get to Olympia at least a month before the Games began. There they continued to train, watched by local officials who could flog or banish any athletes who did not obey instructions. Then, at last, the Games began.

THE FIVE-DAY FESTIVAL

'If you have worked in a manner worthy of coming to Olympia, and have done nothing in an offhand or base way, proceed with good courage; but as for those who have not so exercised, go away wherever you like.'

DAY ONE

Above are the instructions that were given to athletes, their fathers, brothers, and trainers on Day One of the Games. All of them had to swear that they would participate in a fair way. The officials also had to take this oath. And it was up to them to make sure that all the athletes were free-born Greeks (not slaves), and that they had never been accused of **homicide**. Then the competitors entered the stadium and gave their names. In the afternoon the first events took place: running, wrestling, and boxing for boys. The Games were on!

DAYS TWO AND THREE

By the mid-seventh century BC, the second day of the Games was a busy one. It featured the **pentathlon** inside the now-packed stadium, and horse-racing and chariot races in the nearby **hippodrome**. It must have been hard to fit all the pentathlon events in. Some historians think that if an athlete easily won the discus, javelin, and jump, he was judged to be the overall winner without having to run or wrestle.

The Olympic Games were not just a mixture of religion and sport, but also of sport and war. Nowhere was this clearer than in the javelin event. Athletes threw lighter javelins than those used by soldiers, but they were still basically weapons.

Soldiers and athletes alike sometimes attached a little loop of leather. By putting their first finger into the loop they could throw further and more powerfully. ▼

The jump may have been like our modern triple jump – but with a major difference. Jumpers at Olympia launched themselves into the sandpit holding weights, which they used for gaining extra distance in the swing forward.

On the morning of Day Three, it was the ritual to **sacrifice** 100 oxen in honour of Zeus. (The ash of their burnt-up thighs was kept, while the rest of the joints were cooked for a big feast which was held at the end of the Games.) In the afternoon, the running races were held in front of the frenzied stadium crowd. How that crowd must have cheered at the four Games between 164 and 152BC – an all-time great called Leonidas of Rhodes won three crowns at each of them.

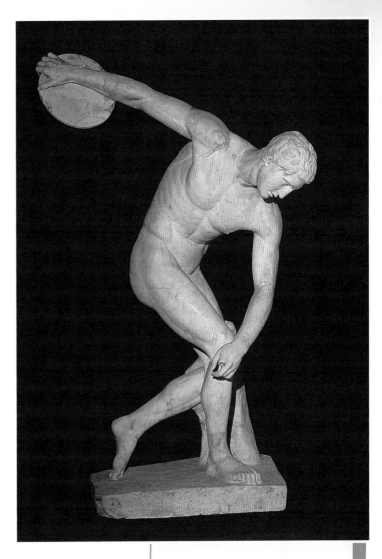

DAYS FOUR AND FIVE

One of the events Leonidas excelled at was the race in armour. This was held on Day Four, as well as all the combat sports – wrestling, boxing and *pankration* (see pages 16–17). Then on Day Five it was time to celebrate. The closing ceremonies included a procession of the winners, followed by their crowning with olive wreaths. After that, it only remained to enjoy the final feast, then go back home and prepare for the next Olympics in four years' time!

After the Games, life-sized victory statues of Olympic champions were made. Unfortunately, very few have survived whole until today – so we have no clear idea what such heroes as Leonidas of Rhodes looked like. But like the image above, the statues would have been wonderful works of art in themselves, showing the athletes' grace and beauty as well as suggesting their great ability.

WOMEN NOT WELCOME

At many sports stadiums today, fans often blow loud horns to add to the excitement. Such sounds during sports events are nothing new. At Olympia, trumpeters gave a blast to signal the start of a race, to call the runners back after a false start, and to announce the winners.

This ancient Greek vase painting shows a soldier blowing a trumpet – as heard at Olympia.

On top of the blasting trumpets, there was the roar of the crowd, trainers shouting from the sidelines and the yells of athletes. But all the noise at the ancient Olympics was made by men. Apart from the priestess and maidens (unmarried women), everyone at the Games was male. Other women were banned as it was thought they would insult the gods. If they were caught they could be put to death. Even women who owned chariots and horses could not watch them compete.

WATCH THAT MAN!

On page 14 you read about the hugely successful combat-sport family of Diagoras of Rhodes. His daughter Kallipateira grew up hearing all about their Olympic victories – and when the time came for her own son to take part, she could not contain her curiosity. Disguised as a male trainer, she slipped into the stadium.

There, to her great delight, she saw her boy Eukles take the boxing crown. Then her delight became a little *too* great: leaping out to embrace the new champion, she blew her own cover! The officials debated what to do with her – and finally let her off, out of respect for her famous family. But from then on trainers had to be as naked as the athletes – to avoid any more confusion!

ANCIENT INTO MODERN

Women were eventually allowed to take part in the Olympics. Some of the first sports they could enter were golf, tennis, and archery. It was not until 1928 that they were allowed to participate in track and field events. Although the number of women competing is still far fewer than men, that number keeps growing.

Now women also take part in more sports. Women competed in the pole-vault and hammer-throwing for the first time at the Sydney Games in 2000. Women's wrestling was included in the 2004 Athens Olympics, and the steeplechase at Beijing in 2008. Women still do not take part in everything. Men-only events include the 20 kilometre and 50 kilometre walk, the decathlon, and the 110 metre hurdles.

Although only men competed in the main Olympic Games, there *were* races for young women at other times. A very old temple to the goddess Hera stood at Olympia. Its officials were in charge of training girl athletes, who then ran short races in the goddess's honour. ▶

THE ROMANS

The Romans invaded Greece in the middle of the 2nd century BC. Greece became part of the great Roman Empire, so things began to change. Although the Romans admired much of the Greek way of life, they were not so sure about Greek sport. For a start, Roman athletes always wore **loincloths**. They were disgusted to see the Greeks compete naked in public. On the other hand, the Romans enjoyed watching public violence so they were happy to bring in more painful sport.

MORE VIOLENCE, PLEASE

The Roman Emperor Nero (who ruled from AD 54-68) was so thrilled by the Greek Games that he actually took part himself at Olympia. By the 4th century AD, more than 150 days each year were set aside for the million or so people living in Rome to enjoy games. Chariot-racing in the Circus Maximus **Hippodrome** was just like the Greek races, with plenty of action and sometimes violence. Romans also liked Greek wrestling, boxing and *pankration* (see pages 16–17) but they also wanted this level of aggression in other sports.

Crowds of over 150,000 people flocked to the great Circus Maximus in Rome and went wild watching four-horse chariot-racing. This picture from the Hollywood film *Ben Hur* shows what a chariot race would have looked like. ▼

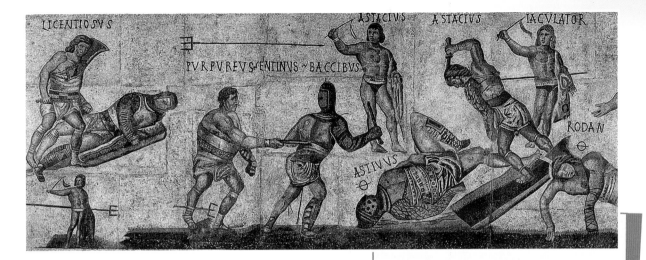

SPORT VERSUS ENTERTAINMENT

The Romans built a great **amphitheatre** that held 150,000 screaming spectators. They paid to watch animals and humans wounded and killed in so-called 'sporting contests'. The Roman view of public sport was really very different from that of the Greeks. The festivals at Olympia were organised, at least at first, for the athletes themselves to test their strength, speed or skill against their fellow competitors. Those in Rome were always staged as **spectacles** for the enjoyment of the public. You could say that, in Greece, sport was mainly about competition. In Rome it was for entertainment.

▲ The Roman public was thrilled by contests between **gladiators** as well as by battles between two armies and their equipment.

And there was another big difference between the two views. For the Greeks, sport and religion went hand-in-hand. Greek athletes competed at Olympia, Nemea, Corinth, and Delphi as a way of honouring their great gods. For several centuries, the Greeks' open-minded masters in Rome let this continue. But all that changed in the 4th century AD, when Christianity became the Empire's official religion. Early Christians were intolerant of any kind of non-Christian worship – and this was probably why, in AD393, the Emperor Theodosius I abolished the Olympic Games altogether.

ALIVE AGAIN

After AD393 there were no more Olympic Games. For hundreds of years they were forgotten about, as well as the names of the Greek champions from long ago. No one knew much about ancient Olympia and what started there. It was not until the 1800s that a new interest in sport began to stir across Europe. In Germany, where gymnastics was becoming very popular, two men – Johann Guts Muths and Ernst Curtius – even suggested reviving the Olympics. In England, a doctor called William Penny Brooks started up local games in 1850. They were like a mini-Olympics for nearby teams. Soon afterwards in Greece, competitive national games were started.

Around 1800 sport began to play a big part in the timetables of private British boys' schools. Favourite sports in Britain, like racing and boxing, were becoming far more organised, and old games like tennis, football, and rugby were given brand new sets of rules which everyone had to follow.

Because the British then had a worldwide Empire, they introduced organised sport to the local people wherever they ruled (including future Olympic host countries such as Australia and Canada). But it was a Frenchman – Baron Pierre de Coubertin – who worked hardest to pick up the Olympic Games where Emperor Theodosius I had forced them to leave off.

◄ Supporters flocked to the first modern Olympic Games in 1896. A brand new stadium was built to host them, in the home of the ancient Olympics – Athens, Greece.

◀ The Olympic flame links ancient to modern. Before each Olympic Games, a torch is lit at Olympia and carried by runners to the Olympic Stadium. In 2006, the torch travelled through seven countries before reaching Turin, Italy.

A NEW AGE

In Paris, in 1892, de Coubertin told everyone his dream: 'Let us export our oarsmen, our runners, our fencers into other lands. That is the true Free Trade of the future; and the day it is introduced into Europe, the cause of Peace will have received a new and strong ally. It inspires me to touch upon another step I now propose … the splendid and **beneficent** task of reviving the Olympic Games.'

After travelling widely in Europe and North America, de Coubertin strongly believed that international sport would be a force for good in the world. At first he found it hard to make other people share his belief. But by 1894 he had won over enough supporters. Plans were laid to stage the first modern Olympic Games in April 1896 – featuring a selection of sports that were popular at that time. And where were they to be held? In Athens – the capital city of Greece, the country that gave birth to the original Olympics.

Victor Duruy, a friend of de Coubertin, once wrote: 'There were splendid festivals, brilliant successes, unforgettable **spectacles**, and at other times vulgarities, disorders, badly arranged ceremonies, and disunited processions.' He was describing the ancient Games, but he could well have been writing about the modern Games that people have now enjoyed since 1896. After all, the Olympic Games in all their history have never been dull. They are usually exciting, and always full of the biggest surprises.

GLOSSARY

alien strange or unfamiliar

amateur someone who competes for fun, rather than as a job, and who is unpaid

amphitheatre circular or oval arena with sloping banks of seats rising around a central open space

archaeologist person who studies ancient history, usually by excavating ancient ruins

beneficent worthwhile, helpful

celeriac a kind of celery

city state an ancient Greek city that was also a little independent country

colony place where people move to in order to live in a new country, while still being ruled from their old country

dressage the art of training a horse in obedience

equestrianism riding or performing on horseback

excavate dig up (often ancient ruins)

founder person who starts something up

gladiator trained performer who fights with a sword or other weapon as a form of entertainment

hippodrome course for chariot and horse races

homicide the killing of one human by another

inscription words written on a monument

legend a story which may or may not be true, usually about a hero

loincloth cloth worn around the waist

myth an ancient story, usually about gods and magical events

pentathlon athletic competition involving five events: running, jumping, wrestling, discus and javelin

periodonikes ancient Greek title meaning a multiple champion at festival Games

precinct enclosed area

professional paid competitor

relief a carving that stands out from the surface of a wall or something similar

sacrifice slaughter of an animal as an offering to a god

sanctuary a place that is recognised as holy

spectacle great public show

thong strip of leather or animal-hide

truce the temporary halting of a war or fight

venison meat that comes from deer

FIND OUT MORE

USING THE INTERNET

Explore the Internet to find out more about the history of the ancient Olympic Games or to see pictures of where they were first held. You can use a search engine such as www.yahooligans.com, or ask a question at www.ask.com. To find out more about the ancient Olympics, you could search by typing in key words such as Olympia, pankration, Theogenes of Thasos, Diagoras of Rhodes, or Milo of Croton.

These are some useful websites to look at to find more information:

http://www.ancientgreece.co.uk/festivals/story/olympics.html
This website has information about the first Games.

http://www.culture.gr/2/21/211/21107a/e211ga02.html
This website shows how Olympia looks today.

http://www.bbc.co.uk/schools/ancientgreece/olympia/olympia1.shtml
This ancient Olympics site is for younger children.

http://www.enchantedlearning.com/olympics/
This website provides general information and activities.

http://www.sikyon.com/Olympia/athletestories_eg.html
Go to this website to find out about famous athletes in ancient Greece.

BOOKS

The Ancient Greek Olympics, Richard Woff (Oxford University Press, 2000)

Welcome to the 776 Olympics!, Jane Bingham (Raintree, 2007)

You Are In: Ancient Greece, Ivan Minnis (Raintree, 2004)

INDEX